DIFFICULT CONVERSATION GUIDE

Rakesh Lazar MBA, PCC (ICF)
Mindset Coach – Communication Confidence

Beyond Skill, Your Success in Communication Depends on Your Mindset and Intent

RAKESH LAZAR

In the dynamic streets of global connections, where my Indian roots mingle with diverse cultural influences, I found myself standing at the crossroads of communication. Visualize a moment during a local festival in Seoul, a convergence of cultures where a simple misinterpretation ignited a series of misunderstandings. It was in this facade of experiences that I uncovered the profound impact that effective communication, or its absence, could wield in our daily lives.

"Beyond Skill, Your Success In Communication Depends On Your Mindset And Intent!" At the heart of this guide lies the belief that true mastery in communication extends beyond skills alone; it's about cultivating the right mindset and intention. Understanding this philosophy will empower you not only to navigate difficult conversations but to do so with empathy, authenticity, and a genuine connection.

This guide doesn't emerge solely from principles but from the crucible of real-life conversations, shaped by a rich fabric of global experiences. Drawing inspiration from interactions worldwide, coaching conversations with senior executives, and insights gained as a Mindset Coach and Design Thinking Mentor, it reflects lessons learned through 15+ years of collaboration in multicultural teams and navigating the challenges of two failed ventures.

Embark on this transformative journey armed with advanced strategies, psychological insights, and practical exercises. Explore the intricacies of advanced communication skills, delve into the psychology of challenging dialogues, and engage in interactive exercises to fortify your learning.

By the end of this guide, you'll not only have acquired advanced communication skills but also gained invaluable insights into preparing your mindset, employing effective communication strategies, managing challenging emotions, and peacefully resolving conflicts. These skills will not only enrich your relationships but also boost your confidence and effectiveness in navigating challenging conversations.

Join us in this transformative voyage, where reading is just the beginning. Actively participate in the exercises and practice the strategies discussed throughout this guide. Your active engagement is the key to unlocking the full potential of this resource.

. . . .

Are you ready to embark on this transformative journey toward mastering difficult conversations with confidence and subtlety?

TABLE OF
Contents

KEY SKILLS & TECHNIQUES

Preparing Your Mindset

Difficult conversations often trigger a range of emotions and can be challenging. Preparing your mindset is the first step in navigating these conversations effectively. Here's how you can do it:

A. Cultivate an Open and Non-Judgmental Mindset:

Approaching a difficult conversation with an open and non-judgmental mindset is crucial. This mindset allows you to create a safe space for open dialogue and fosters a sense of trust.

During my time at SolBridge International School of Business (South Korea), I was entrusted with organizing a business case competition with teams from 40 diverse nationalities. In the midst of the intense preparation week, a team approached me with a crucial question: What's the key to success beyond intellectual preparation? This inquiry became the catalyst for understanding that success isn't solely about brilliant ideas; it's equally rooted in effective communication. Navigating cultural nuances, practicing empathetic communication, and fostering collaboration emerged as the essential components—the X-factor—for mindset preparation.

☑ **Practical guidance:**
  ◉ **Create Safe Spaces:** Foster an environment where open dialogue is encouraged, allowing trust to flourish.

- ◉ **Learn from Diverse Experiences:** Draw inspiration from diverse situations, like navigating cultural nuances and fostering collaboration, to develop an open mindset.

B. Acknowledge Your Emotions and Biases:

Recognize that you're human and, like everyone else, you have emotions and biases. It's normal to feel a range of emotions before and during a difficult conversation, such as fear, anger, or frustration.

As emotions ran high during the competition, team members acknowledged the impact of their individual emotions and biases on decision-making. By openly discussing these factors, they dismantled potential barriers to effective communication. This acknowledgment facilitated a deeper understanding of each team member's perspective and laid the groundwork for constructive dialogue.

- ✓ **Practical guidance:**
  - ◉ **Normalizing Emotions:** Understand that experiencing emotions like fear and frustration is normal, acknowledging their existence.
  - ◉ **Transparent Communication:** Encourage open discussions about emotions and biases to dismantle potential communication barriers

C. Understand the Impact of Emotions:

Emotions play a significant role in conversations, especially difficult ones. They can affect your behavior, tone, and even your ability to listen effectively. Understanding this impact is essential.

Through this experience, the team grasped the significant role emotions played in their interactions. They learned to identify emotional triggers and proactively manage them. This newfound understanding not only improved their intra-team dynamics but also enhanced their ability to navigate discussions with judges effectively.

EXPLORE HOW EMOTIONS INFLUENCE CONVERSATIONS:

Consider how your emotions, as well as the emotions of the other person, can shape the dialogue. Recognize that emotions can either facilitate understanding or hinder it.

LEARN TECHNIQUES TO MANAGE EMOTIONS:

Delve into techniques that help you manage your emotions during challenging conversations. This might include deep breathing, mindfulness exercises, or self-regulation strategies. These techniques can help you stay calm and composed, even when emotions run high.

CREATE A CONDUCIVE ATMOSPHERE:

Emotions are contagious. Your emotional state can influence the atmosphere of the conversation. By managing your emotions, you can contribute to a more relaxed and constructive environment.

Remember, preparing your mindset is not about suppressing emotions but about acknowledging and managing them effectively. It's the foundation for constructive communication during difficult conversations.

Define Your Purpose

Before you embark on a difficult conversation, it's crucial to clarify your purpose and objectives. Your intentions and desired outcomes should guide the conversation. Here's how you can do it effectively:

A.   Clarify Your Intentions and Desired Outcomes:

Take time to reflect on what you aim to achieve through this conversation. Drawing inspiration from a historical context, let's look at the remarkable story of the Marshall Plan:

In the aftermath of World War II, Europe was devastated, both economically and socially. The Marshall Plan, officially known as the European Recovery Program, was initiated by the United States in 1948. The purpose was clear – to provide massive financial assistance to help rebuild European economies and prevent the spread of communism.

This monumental initiative was fueled by a well-defined intention – to foster economic recovery, political stability, and overall well-being. The objectives were explicit – allocate funds for infrastructure, encourage trade, and establish a foundation for lasting peace. The Marshall Plan wasn't merely a conversation; it was a strategic effort with a defined purpose.

Reflecting on the Marshall Plan, consider the transformative impact that clear intentions and well-defined objectives can have. While the scale differs, the principle remains the same – approaching a conversation with a distinct purpose lays the groundwork for constructive outcomes.

   ✅ **Practical Guidance:** Write down your objectives. This can serve as a mental anchor during the conversation, helping you stay on track and focused on your goals. Ensure your intentions are clear, honest, and aligned with a positive outcome. Avoid hidden agendas or ulterior motives, as they can hinder trust and open communication.

B.   Focus on Mutual Understanding, Not Winning:

Shift your mindset from a competitive "winning" approach to a collaborative one focused on mutual understanding. For this, let's draw inspiration from the Cuban Missile Crisis:

During the Cuban Missile Crisis in 1962, the United States and the Soviet Union found themselves on the brink of nuclear war. President John F. Kennedy's approach wasn't centered on 'winning' the conversation but on understanding the Soviet perspective and finding common ground. The objective was clear – prevent a nuclear catastrophe and maintain global peace.

The crisis demanded a shift in mindset, emphasizing mutual understanding over victory. Kennedy's leadership during this tense period showcased the power of collaborative intent in the face of adversity.

   ✅ **Practical Guidance:** Apply this historical lesson to your own difficult conversations.

      ◉ Remind yourself before and during the conversation that your goal is to foster understanding and cooperation, not to prove yourself right. This mindset shift can significantly impact the tone and outcome of the discussion.

- ⊙ Understand that a difficult conversation is not a debate or argument to be won. It's an opportunity to connect, learn, and find common ground.

C.   Foster Emotional Intelligence:

Emotional intelligence (EI) is the ability to recognize, understand, and manage your own emotions and the emotions of others. Let's draw from the life of Nelson Mandela:

Nelson Mandela, the iconic leader of the anti-apartheid movement, demonstrated exceptional emotional intelligence during the negotiations to end apartheid. Mandela's ability to understand and manage his emotions, along with acknowledging the emotions of his adversaries, played a pivotal role in achieving a peaceful transition to majority rule.

- ✓ **Practical Guidance:** Embrace the wisdom of leaders like Mandela. Before the conversation, engage in self-reflection. Recognize your emotional state and its potential impact on the discussion. If you're feeling anxious or upset, consider how to manage these emotions constructively.

  - ⊙ Develop your EI by practicing self-awareness, self-regulation, empathy, and social skills.

  - ⊙ During the conversation, pay attention to the other person's emotions. Listen actively and empathetically, acknowledging their feelings and validating their perspective.

D.   Setting SMART Goals for Conversations:

Applying the SMART framework to your conversation goals makes them clearer and more attainable. Let's draw inspiration from the Apollo 11 mission:

The Apollo 11 mission, which successfully landed humans on the Moon in 1969, was driven by SMART goals. NASA's mission was Specific – land astronauts on the Moon, Measurable – gather samples and conduct

✓ **Practical Guidance:** Like the Apollo 11 mission, set specific, measurable, achievable, relevant, and time-bound goals for your difficult conversations. This structured approach enhances clarity and success.

By weaving these historical narratives into the fabric of "Defining Your Purpose," we emphasize the transformative impact that a clear purpose can have on the outcomes of difficult conversations.

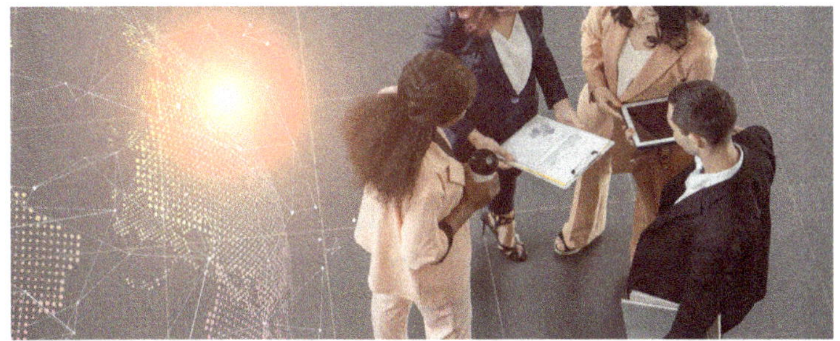

Effective Communication Strategies

Difficult conversations often require a higher level of communication skill to navigate successfully. In this section, we will explore specific techniques and strategies that empower you to communicate effectively in challenging dialogues. Each strategy is accompanied by practical guidance and illustrative examples:

A. Active Listening:

Active listening is a foundational communication skill. When engaging in difficult conversations, employ these practical steps to actively listen:

a. **Give Your Full Attention:** Make a conscious effort to be fully present during the conversation. Minimize distractions, put away electronic devices, and maintain eye contact with the speaker.

b. **Use Verbal Cues:** Show your engagement by using verbal cues like nodding and saying "I understand" or "I see" to let the speaker know you're actively listening.

c. **Paraphrase and Reflect:** Periodically paraphrase what the speaker has said to ensure you've understood correctly. Reflect their feelings and concerns to demonstrate empathy.

d. **Ask Open-Ended Questions:** Encourage the speaker to share more by asking open-ended questions that require more than a simple "yes" or "no" response.

Consider a situation where a coworker expresses frustration about a project. Active listening would involve giving your full attention, summarizing their concerns, and asking open-ended questions to delve deeper.

Coworker ➜ *"I'm really frustrated with how this project is going. It feels like we're not making any progress."*

You (Active Listening) ➜ *"I hear your frustration about the project. Can you tell me more about what specifically is causing these challenges?"*

Practice Active Listening – Now that you've gained insights into the art of active listening, it's time to put theory into action. Engage in a real-world scenario to refine your skills:

Exercise: Choose a podcast or initiate a conversation with a friend. Challenge yourself to practice active listening actively. Summarize the main points, ask open-ended questions, and take note of your observations.

Want to take it a step further? Utilize the provided **Active Listening Worksheet** (pg. 57⬀) in the consolidated section for a structured reflection on your experience. Jot down your thoughts, identify areas for improvement, and track your progress.

Remember, true mastery comes from practice. Head to the consolidated section for more exercises and worksheets to enhance your communication and conflict resolution skills. Happy practicing!

B.   Non-Verbal Communication:

Non-verbal cues play a significant role in conveying your message. In difficult conversations, follow these practical steps to ensure your non-verbal communication aligns with your intended message:

a. **Maintain an Open Posture:** Keep your body language open and approachable, avoiding crossed arms or defensive postures.

b. **Make Eye Contact:** Sustained, friendly eye contact communicates attentiveness and empathy.

c. **Use Calm and Even Tone:** Speak in a calm and even tone, avoiding raised voices or accusatory language.

* * * * * * * * * * * * *

When discussing sensitive topics, maintaining an open posture, making eye contact, and using a calm tone can signal empathy and receptivity.

You (Non-Verbal Communication) ➜ During a conversation about a project delay, you maintain an open posture, make eye contact with your colleague, and speak in a calm and even tone, showing understanding and empathy.

C. Tone of Voice:

The tone in which you speak can impact the emotional tone of the conversation. To manage your tone effectively during difficult conversations, consider the following practical steps:

a. **Reflect on the Emotional Context:** Before speaking, take a moment to gauge the emotional context of the conversation. Are emotions running high? Is the atmosphere tense? Adjust your tone accordingly.

b. **Modulate Your Tone:** Strive to keep your tone neutral and calm, especially when addressing sensitive issues. Avoid accusatory or harsh tones that can escalate emotions.

c. **Use "I" Statements:** Frame your statements using "I" instead of "you" to express your feelings and perspective without sounding confrontational.

When addressing a mistake, a gentle and non-accusatory tone can make it easier for the other person to accept feedback and work towards a solution.

You (Tone of Voice) → *When discussing a mistake made by a team member, you maintain a calm and non-accusatory tone, saying, "I noticed an error in the report, and I think we can work together to find a solution."*

Managing Difficult Emotions

While recognizing and managing emotions is crucial, this section delves deeper by addressing specific emotions frequently encountered in challenging conversations, such as anger, defensiveness, and anxiety. We will provide you with practical strategies to manage these emotions constructively, fostering a calm and productive dialogue.

A. Managing Anger:

Anger can be a powerful and often disruptive emotion in difficult conversations.

To manage anger effectively, consider the lessons from the Civil Rights Movement in the United States:

During the Civil Rights Movement, activists faced immense anger and resistance while striving for racial equality. Dr. Martin Luther King Jr. exemplified a strategic approach, emphasizing nonviolent communication and understanding. His leadership showed that managing anger requires both courage and a commitment to constructive dialogue.

a. **Recognize It:** Acknowledge when anger arises within you or the other person. Understanding its presence is the first step to managing it.

b. **Take a Pause:** When anger flares, it's beneficial to take a pause. Step away from the conversation if necessary to cool down and regain composure.

c. **Express Without Blame:** When expressing anger, use "I" statements to communicate your feelings without blaming or accusing the other person.

d. **Practice Active Listening:** If the other person is angry, practice active listening to show that you understand their perspective, even if you don't agree.

• • • • • • • • • • • • •

In a team meeting, John expresses frustration about a decision that affects the project's direction. He says, "I can't believe we're changing the project scope again. This is ridiculous." In response, Mary, the team leader, recognizes his anger and replies, "I can see that you're really frustrated by this. I want to understand why."

B. Handling Defensiveness:

Defensiveness is a common response in difficult conversations and can hinder constructive dialogue.

Learn from the fall of the Berlin Wall:

• • • • • • • • • • • • •

As the Berlin Wall fell in 1989, symbolizing the end of the Cold War, it required leaders on both sides to navigate complex emotions. The ability to resist defensiveness and embrace dialogue played a crucial role in peaceful reunification.

a. **Stay Open-Minded:** When faced with defensiveness, remind yourself to stay open-minded and receptive to the other person's viewpoint.

b.   **Use Empathetic Statements:** Express empathy and understanding to reduce defensiveness. For instance, "I can see why you might feel that way."

c.   **Ask Clarifying Questions:** Encourage the other person to share more about their concerns and perspective. This can reduce defensiveness by making them feel heard.

d.   **Avoid Blame:** Refrain from placing blame or making accusatory statements, which can trigger defensiveness.

If a colleague becomes defensive when discussing a missed deadline, you can say, "I want to understand what led to the delay. Can you share your perspective?"

During a performance review, Sarah, an employee, becomes defensive when her manager, Mark, points out areas for improvement. Sarah says, "I've been doing my best, and now you're telling me I'm not meeting expectations?" Mark remains open-minded and asks, "I want to understand your perspective better. Can you share more about your concerns?"

C.   Managing Anxiety:

Anxiety can make difficult conversations even more challenging.

Gain inspiration from the "Little Rock Nine" during the desegregation of Central High School in 1957:

The "Little Rock Nine" faced tremendous anxiety as they bravely integrated a previously all-white school. Their courage and preparation in the face of intense opposition serve as a reminder that managing anxiety involves resilience and careful planning.

a.   **Control Your Breathing:** Deep, slow breaths can help calm anxiety and maintain focus during the conversation.

b. **Use Positive Self-Talk:** Counter anxious thoughts with positive self-talk. Remind yourself that you are prepared and capable of handling the conversation.

c. **Plan and Prepare:** Thoroughly prepare for the conversation by outlining your points and anticipating responses. This can boost your confidence and reduce anxiety.

d. **Accept Imperfection:** Understand that not every conversation will go perfectly. It's okay to make mistakes and learn from them.

• • • • • • • • • • • •

Before a difficult conversation with a colleague about a project delay, Jessica feels anxious. She takes a moment to control her breathing, reminding herself that she is prepared for the conversation. During the dialogue, she feels more confident and maintains her composure.

This section empowers you with strategies to navigate and manage specific emotions that often arise in difficult conversations. By addressing these emotions constructively, you can maintain a calm and productive demeanor, fostering more positive outcomes.

Practice Emotional Self-Regulation – Now that you've explored the significance of emotional self-regulation, let's put it into practice. Choose a real-life scenario to refine your emotional self-regulation skills:

Exercise: Recall a recent situation that triggered strong emotions. Challenge yourself to practice emotional self-regulation actively. Utilize deep breathing, mindfulness exercises, or relaxation techniques to manage your emotions and strive to maintain a calm demeanor.

Want to enhance your learning further? Utilize the provided Emotional Self-Regulation Worksheet (pg. 60⬏) in the consolidated section for a structured reflection on your experience. Jot down your observations, assess the effectiveness of your self-regulation strategies, and monitor your progress.

Remember, true mastery comes from practice. Head to the consolidated section for more exercises and worksheets to strengthen your communication and conflict resolution skills. Happy practicing!

Dealing with Resistance and Opposition

Difficult conversations may encounter resistance, opposition, or defensiveness from the other party involved. In this section, we will discuss effective techniques for managing such situations, defusing tension, and creating a more collaborative and productive atmosphere.

A.   Recognizing Resistance:

Recognizing resistance is the first step in addressing it. Look for signs such as defensiveness, avoidance, or a lack of engagement in the conversation.

In the bustling offices of a tech startup named InnovateX, a team was working on a revolutionary project codenamed "Project Phoenix." The project aimed to redefine the company's product line and set new industry standards. However, as deadlines loomed, tensions soared. One team member, Alex, began avoiding discussions about a critical performance issue hindering Project Phoenix. The signs of resistance were subtle but noticeable.

B.   Active Listening and Empathy:

Use active listening and empathy to demonstrate your understanding of the other person's perspective.

a.   **Reflect Their Concerns:** Paraphrase and reflect the concerns or objections raised by the other party. This shows that you value their viewpoint.

b.   **Acknowledge Their Emotions:** Recognize and validate their emotions. Understanding their feelings can reduce resistance.

C.   Clarify and Seek Solutions:

Clarify misunderstandings and seek collaborative solutions. Encourage the other party to share their perspective and work together to find common ground.

a.   **Ask Open-Ended Questions:** Encourage the other party to share more about their concerns, allowing them to express themselves fully.

b.   **Brainstorm Solutions:** Explore potential solutions together, emphasizing a shared problem-solving approach.

D.   Set Clear Expectations:

Define clear expectations and agreements to minimize future resistance. Ensure that both parties understand their roles and responsibilities.

After reaching an agreement on modifications to Project Phoenix, Sarah documented the resolutions, ensuring both parties had a clear understanding of their roles and responsibilities.

a. **Document Agreements:** If a resolution is reached, document it, and ensure that both parties have a clear understanding of the agreed-upon actions.

E.   Maintain Respect and Professionalism:

Maintain a respectful and professional tone throughout the conversation, even when faced with resistance. Avoid engaging in confrontations or escalating tension.

Throughout the conversation, Sarah maintained a respectful tone, using "I" statements to express her perspective without blaming Alex. This approach prevented confrontation and upheld professionalism.

a. **Use "I" Statements:** Express your own perspective without assigning blame. Avoid phrases like "You should have…" or "You're wrong."

F.   Know When to Escalate:

Sometimes, despite your efforts, the resistance may persist. Know when it's appropriate to escalate the matter to a higher authority or mediator.

Despite their efforts, some resistance persisted. Sarah, keeping a record of their conversation, decided it was time to escalate the matter to higher management to ensure a swift resolution.

a. **Maintain a Record:** Keep a record of the conversation and any agreements reached. This documentation may be useful in the event of further escalation.

By employing these techniques and strategies, you can effectively manage resistance, opposition, or defensiveness during difficult conversations and create a more collaborative and constructive atmosphere. Recognizing the signs of resistance and applying these approaches will enhance the chances of reaching a resolution.

Building Rapport and Trust

Building and maintaining rapport and trust during difficult conversations is fundamental to achieving positive outcomes. In this section, we will explore the significance of trust, how it is established, maintained, and rebuilt when compromised, and offer practical advice for creating an environment of trust.

A.   Understanding the Importance of Trust:

Trust is the foundation of any productive conversation. Begin by acknowledging the role that trust plays in effective communication. Recognize that a lack of trust can lead to skepticism, defensiveness, and an uncooperative atmosphere during the conversation.

As a coach, navigating the intricate landscape of challenging conversations with my clients is a journey I embrace with dedication. During a coaching engagement with my client in Kuala Lumpur, Ahmad, grappling with trust issues surfacing in a high-stakes decision-making meeting regarding resource allocation for a new software, became the focal point of our exploration.

B. Building Trust Through Transparency:

Transparency is a key component of trust-building. Encourage open and honest communication.

Guided by insights shared in our coaching sessions, Ahmad, recognizing the cultural dynamics at play in Malaysian business settings, openly divulged the reasons behind a project delay. This act created an environment where team members felt heard and respected. Active listening, a principle we frequently discuss, came into play as Ahmad demonstrated that the perspectives of his team were not only acknowledged but genuinely valued.

    a.   **Share Information:** Share relevant information and be transparent about your intentions and expectations in the conversation.

    b.   **Active Listening:** Actively listen to the other person, demonstrating that their perspective is valued.

C. Empathy and Understanding:

Empathy is a powerful tool for building trust. Show understanding and compassion for the other person's feelings and viewpoint.

In navigating the frustration among culturally diverse team members, Ahmad, embodying the empathetic approach we champion in our coaching, acknowledged their emotions and expressed genuine concern for the conversation's impact on the team. The importance of recognizing the emotions of others and validating their feelings took center stage. Genuine concern for the impact of difficult conversations on others became a cornerstone of Ahmad's approach.

    a.   **Acknowledge Emotions:** Recognize the emotions the other person is experiencing and validate their feelings.

    b.   **Express Concern:** Show genuine concern for the impact of the conversation on the other person.

D. Consistency and Reliability:

Consistency in your words and actions is essential for trust-building. Always follow through on commitments and promises.

Ahmad's commitment to following through on commitments and promises became instrumental. Honoring agreements and providing timely feedback, Ahmad, influenced by our coaching insights, restored trust that had momentarily wavered.

a. **Honor Agreements:** If you agree to take specific actions, ensure you follow through within the agreed-upon timeframe.

b. **Be Predictable:** Strive to maintain a consistent approach to communication and decision-making.

E. Rebuilding Trust:

Trust may be compromised in some difficult conversations. Explore strategies for rebuilding trust in such cases.

Strategies for rebuilding trust, a subject we explore in depth, came to Ahmad's aid. In the aftermath of suspicions, Ahmad initiated apologies, took responsibility for any misunderstandings, and showcased commitment to change by setting new guidelines.

a. **Apologize and Take Responsibility:** If you or the other party played a role in damaging trust, take responsibility and offer a sincere apology.

b. **Demonstrate Change:** Show through your actions that you are committed to rebuilding trust. This may involve setting clear expectations and boundaries.

 Creating a Trusting Environment:

Beyond individual actions, consider the overall environment in your organization or relationship.

In the wake of this trust-rebuilding journey, Ahmad, fostered a culture where trust was not just valued but prioritized. Channels for open and honest feedback were established. Encouraging a culture where trust is cherished and given priority became a focal point of Ahmad's leadership.

a. **Foster a Culture of Trust:** Encourage a culture where trust is valued and prioritized.

b. **Open Channels for Feedback:** Create opportunities for open and honest feedback, allowing concerns to be addressed promptly.

By understanding the importance of trust, employing transparency, empathy, and consistency, and being prepared to rebuild trust, when necessary, you can create an environment conducive to productive and positive outcomes in difficult conversations. Trust is the bridge to effective communication and understanding, even in the most challenging situations.

Effective Problem-Solving and Decision-Making

In difficult conversations, effective problem-solving and decision-making are pivotal for achieving mutually agreeable resolutions. This section provides a structured framework for addressing issues, generating solutions, and making informed decisions collaboratively.

A. Identifying Issues and Concerns:

The first step in effective problem-solving is identifying the issues and concerns at hand. Encourage open and honest dialogue to uncover the root causes of the problem.

a.   **Active Listening:** Actively listen to the other party's concerns and ask open-ended questions to gain a comprehensive understanding of the issues.

b.   **Paraphrase and Clarify:** Reflect and paraphrase the concerns to ensure clarity and alignment on the problems.

Imagine you are a part of the leadership team in a longstanding organization facing a challenging decision. The team is grappling with the need to lay off a top executive who has been with the company for two decades. Despite the executive's historical contributions, recent years have seen a decline in performance, leading to concerns about the individual's impact on the organization.

B.   Generating Solutions Collaboratively:

Collaboration is key to generating effective solutions. Promote a spirit of working together to address the identified problems.

1. **Brainstorm Solutions:** Encourage both parties to brainstorm potential solutions without judgment.

2. **Evaluate and Prioritize:** Assess the proposed solutions based on feasibility, impact, and alignment with objectives.

In response to the identified concerns, the leadership team, engages in a collaborative brainstorming session. You consider various solutions, including providing targeted support and coaching, restructuring the executive's role, or, as a last resort, initiating a well-managed transition.

C.   Making Informed Decisions:

Making informed decisions requires a systematic approach that considers the pros and cons of each solution.

1. **Gather Information:** Collect relevant data, opinions, and insights to inform the decision-making process.

2. **Assess Risks and Benefits:** Evaluate the potential risks and benefits of each solution. Consider short-term and long-term implications.

The leadership team, conducts a thorough analysis, seeking input from HR, performance records, and external consultants. You carefully weigh the potential impacts on the executive, the team, and the organization as a whole.

D.   Consensus and Agreement:

Strive to reach consensus or mutual agreement on the selected solution. This ensures that both parties are committed to the resolution.

1. **Clarify Roles and Responsibilities:** Define the roles and responsibilities of each party in implementing the solution.

2. **Document the Agreement:** Record the agreed-upon solution, roles, and expected outcomes to avoid future misunderstandings.

E.   Follow-Up and Evaluation:

After implementing the chosen solution, follow up to evaluate its effectiveness. This step ensures that the resolution remains sustainable.

1. **Set Evaluation Periods:** Establish timeframes for reviewing the outcomes and effectiveness of the chosen solution.

2. **Adjust as Needed:** If the solution does not yield the expected results, be open to adjustments and further problem-solving.

This framework for effective problem-solving and decision-making emphasizes collaboration and resolution in difficult conversations. By actively identifying issues, generating solutions together, making informed decisions, reaching consensus, and evaluating outcomes, you can achieve productive resolutions that benefit all parties involved.

Practice Problem-Solving Scenarios – As you delve into the intricacies of problem-solving, let's apply theory to practice. Engage in problem-solving exercises that mirror real-life scenarios, allowing you to sharpen your skills in a practical setting:

Exercise: Collaborate with a partner or a group to tackle problem-solving scenarios. Identify issues collectively, generate potential solutions, and make informed decisions to simulate real-life problem-solving.

Want to take it a step further? Utilize the provided Problem-Solving Scenarios Worksheet (pg. 63⊘) in the consolidated section. This worksheet will assist you in outlining scenarios, recording potential solutions, and evaluating the decision-making process.

Remember, problem-solving is an art perfected through practice. Head to the consolidated section for more exercises and worksheets to hone your communication and conflict resolution skills. Happy practicing!

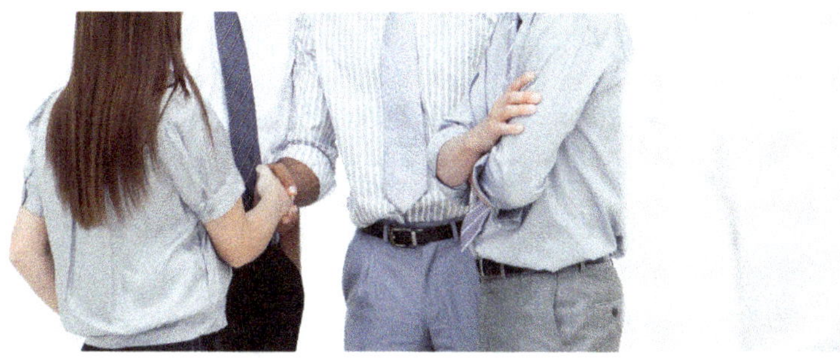

Handling Different Personalities

In the realm of difficult conversations, understanding and adapting to different personality types is essential for productive communication. This section delves into strategies for tailoring your approach to engage effectively with a variety of personalities.

A. Recognizing Personality Types:

The first step in handling different personalities is recognizing the diverse traits and characteristics of individuals you might encounter.

    a. **Observe Behaviors:** Pay attention to how people behave and communicate during the conversation. This can provide clues about their personality type.

    b. **Use Personality Assessments:** Familiarize yourself with personality assessment tools like the Myers-Briggs Type Indicator (MBTI) or the DiSC model to understand common personality traits.

During a team meeting, notice that some team members are more assertive and outspoken, while others are reserved and contemplative.

B.   Tailoring Your Communication Style:

Once you recognize different personality types, adapt your communication style accordingly to establish rapport and effective communication.

a.   **Adjust Your Tone:** Match your tone and energy level to the individual's preferences. For example, be more enthusiastic with outgoing personalities and calmer with introverted individuals.

b.   **Modify Your Approach:** Tailor your approach to align with their communication style. If someone is detail-oriented, provide specific information, while with a big-picture thinker, emphasize broader concepts.

When discussing a project update with a detail-oriented team member, provide them with specific data and facts. For a colleague who prefers a big-picture perspective, focus on the project's overall progress.

C.   Adapting to Communication Preferences:

Understanding and accommodating individual communication preferences can lead to more successful interactions.

a.   **Listen Actively:** Pay attention to their communication style and respond accordingly. If someone values data and facts, provide them with evidence to support your points.

b.   **Use Visual Aids:** Utilize visual aids, charts, or diagrams when communicating with individuals who are more visually oriented.

When discussing financial reports with a visual thinker, incorporate graphs and charts to illustrate key data points.

D. Empathy and Flexibility:

Approach each conversation with empathy and flexibility. Recognize that people may have unique needs and communication styles.

a. **Practice Empathy:** Try to understand and validate the emotions and perspectives of the other person.

b. **Be Open to Feedback:** If someone provides feedback about your communication style, be open to making adjustments.

If a team member mentions that they prefer more concise communication, adapt your style to provide more concise updates.

E. Dealing with Conflict:

In situations where different personalities clash, employ conflict resolution techniques and mediation to find common ground.

a. **Seek Common Goals:** Identify shared objectives and interests to align the conversation toward a common purpose.

b. **Use a Mediator:** In cases of significant personality conflicts, consider involving a neutral mediator to facilitate the conversation.

In a project meeting where two team members with contrasting personalities clash, a mediator can help them find common ground by focusing on the project's success.

Understanding and adapting to different personalities is a skill that can greatly enhance the effectiveness of your communication during difficult conversations. By recognizing and adjusting to individual preferences, you can foster more harmonious and productive interactions.

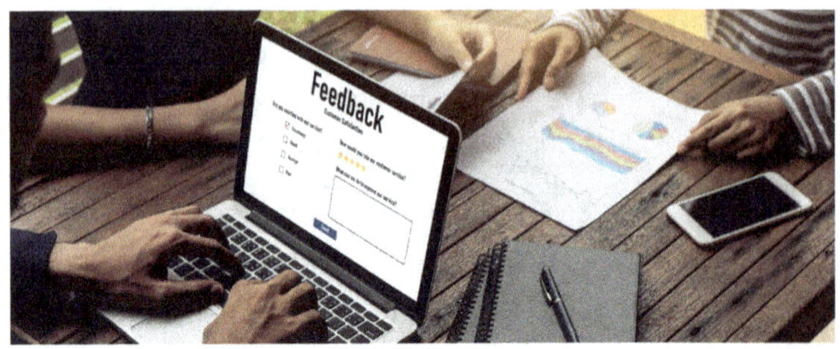

Giving and Receiving Feedback

In the context of difficult conversations, the ability to give and receive feedback is a critical skill. This section explores the art of offering constructive feedback and provides strategies for accepting feedback with an open mind.

A. Giving Constructive Feedback:

Constructive feedback is essential for improvement and conflict resolution. Here's how to offer feedback effectively:

a.   **Be Specific and Focused:** Address specific behaviors or issues rather than making general criticisms.

b.   **Use "I" Statements:** Frame your feedback in terms of your observations and feelings, e.g., "I noticed that..." or "I felt..."

When providing feedback to a colleague about a missed deadline, you can say, "I observed that the project deadline wasn't met, and I felt concerned about its impact."

B.   Avoid Blame and Judgment:

To ensure the feedback is well-received, avoid placing blame or making judgments.

   a.   **Focus on Behavior:** Address the actions or behaviors that need improvement, not the person's character or intentions.

   b.   **Use Non-inflammatory Language:** Keep your language neutral and avoid making accusations.

Instead of saying, "You're always careless with your work," say, "I've noticed some errors in your recent reports that we need to address."

C.   Offer Solutions or Suggestions:

Provide potential solutions or suggestions for improvement when giving feedback.

   a.   **Problem-Solving Approach:** Encourage a collaborative approach to resolving the issue by suggesting possible solutions.

   b.   **Ask for Input:** Invite the other party to share their ideas for improvement.

After giving feedback about communication issues in a team, suggest holding regular team meetings to improve information sharing and ask for their input.

D.   Receiving Feedback with an Open Mind:

Being receptive to feedback is crucial for personal and professional growth. Here's how to accept feedback with an open mind:

   a.   **Listen Actively:** Pay full attention to the feedback without interrupting or becoming defensive.

   b.   **Ask Clarifying Questions:** Seek clarification if you don't fully understand the feedback.

E.   Avoid Defensiveness:

Resist the urge to become defensive when receiving feedback.

    a.   **Stay Calm:** Maintain a composed demeanor and focus on the feedback itself, rather than your emotional reaction.

    b.   **Reflect on the Feedback:** Take some time to reflect on the feedback provided before responding.

F.   Express Gratitude:

Show appreciation for the feedback, regardless of whether it was positive or challenging.

    a.   **Thank the Person:** Express gratitude for their willingness to provide feedback and their desire for improvement.

G. Follow-Up and Action:

When you receive feedback, take action to address the issues discussed.

a. **Set Goals for Improvement:** Establish goals and a plan for addressing the feedback.

b. **Provide Updates:** Keep the person who provided feedback informed of your progress.

If you receive feedback about your time management skills, set specific goals to improve and periodically update your progress with the individual.

Giving and receiving feedback is a vital aspect of personal and professional growth, and it plays a crucial role in resolving conflicts. By offering constructive feedback and accepting it with an open mind, you can build stronger relationships and continually improve your communication and interpersonal skills.

Practice Feedback Exchange – Constructive feedback is a cornerstone of effective communication. Now, it's time to put your knowledge into action. Engage in feedback exchange with a partner to refine your skills:

Exercise: Pair up with a friend or colleague and take turns giving and receiving feedback on a specific topic or situation. Utilize the guidelines from this guide for constructive feedback to ensure a meaningful exchange.

Looking to enhance your feedback exchange experience? Utilize the provided Feedback Exchange Worksheet (pg. 66) in the consolidated section for a structured reflection on your feedback conversations. Document key points, note areas for improvement, and track your progress.

Remember, feedback is a two-way street. Head to the consolidated section for more exercises and worksheets to amplify your communication and conflict resolution skills. Happy practicing!

Cultural Sensitivity and Diversity

In an increasingly diverse and interconnected world, cultural sensitivity is crucial when engaging in difficult conversations. This section underscores the importance of recognizing and respecting cultural differences in communication and offers practical guidance on navigating conversations with people from diverse backgrounds.

A. Understanding Cultural Sensitivity:

Cultural sensitivity involves recognizing and respecting the values, norms, and practices of different cultures. Start by understanding what cultural sensitivity means:

a. **Cultural Awareness:** Develop an awareness of different cultures and the impact of culture on communication styles.

b. **Avoid Stereotyping:** Recognize that individuals from the same culture can have diverse beliefs and behaviors.

When dealing with international clients, educate yourself about their cultural customs, such as greetings, business practices, and communication etiquette.

B. Navigating Cultural Differences:

Navigating cultural differences involves adapting your communication to honor the values and norms of others.

    a.   **Active Listening:** Pay close attention to the cultural cues and nuances in the conversation.

    b.   **Respect Personal Space:** Be mindful of cultural differences in personal space and physical contact.

When conversing with a colleague from a culture that values a reserved personal space, maintain a comfortable distance during the conversation.

C. Avoid Cultural Assumptions:

Avoid making assumptions about an individual's beliefs or practices based on their cultural background.

    a.   **Ask for Clarification:** If you're unsure about someone's cultural preferences, politely ask for their input.

    b.   **Learn from Others:** Engage in conversations with people from diverse backgrounds to learn about their experiences and perspectives.

If you're working on a project with a colleague from a different culture, ask them if there are any specific cultural considerations or preferences you should be aware of.

D.   Respect and Inclusivity:

Promote an inclusive environment where all voices are heard and respected.

a.   **Embrace Diversity:** Celebrate diversity as a source of strength in the conversation.

b.   **Avoid Bias:** Ensure that no one is marginalized or treated unfairly based on their cultural background.

• • • • • • • • • • • • •

During a team meeting with diverse members, encourage all team members to share their perspectives and be respectful of cultural differences.

E.   Language and Communication Styles:

Recognize that language and communication styles can vary significantly across cultures.

a.   **Use Plain Language:** When communicating across language barriers, use plain and clear language to ensure understanding.

b.   **Be Patient:** Be patient and allow time for individuals from non-native English-speaking backgrounds to express themselves.

• • • • • • • • • • • • •

When working with a team member who has language barriers, communicate clearly and encourage them to ask questions if they need clarification.

F.   Conflict Resolution in Cross-Cultural Contexts:

In the event of conflicts or disagreements, approach resolution with cultural sensitivity.

a.   **Understand Conflict Styles:** Recognize that individuals from different cultures may have varying approaches to conflict resolution.

b. **Seek Common Ground:** Strive to find common ground and solutions that respect the values and norms of all parties involved.

If a conflict arises during a negotiation with international partners, acknowledge the cultural differences in conflict resolution styles and work towards a mutually acceptable solution.

By emphasizing cultural sensitivity and diversity in communication, you can build stronger relationships, foster inclusivity, and create an environment where individuals from various cultural backgrounds feel valued and respected during difficult conversations. Understanding and respecting cultural differences is essential for effective and harmonious communication.

Cultural Sensitivity Reflection – Navigating diverse cultural landscapes is integral to effective communication. Now, let's apply this understanding to your experiences:

Exercise: Reflect on a recent interaction with someone from a different cultural background. Consider the cultural nuances and communication styles that were at play during the conversation. Challenge yourself to recognize and appreciate the diversity in communication.

Want to delve deeper into your cultural sensitivity reflections? Utilize the provided Cultural Sensitivity Reflection Worksheet (pg. 69⬿) in the consolidated section for a structured documentation of your experiences. Jot down your reflections, recognize cultural differences, and identify opportunities for improvement.

Remember, cultural sensitivity is a continuous journey. Head to the consolidated section for more exercises and worksheets to enrich your communication and conflict resolution skills. Happy practicing!

Conflict Resolution Models

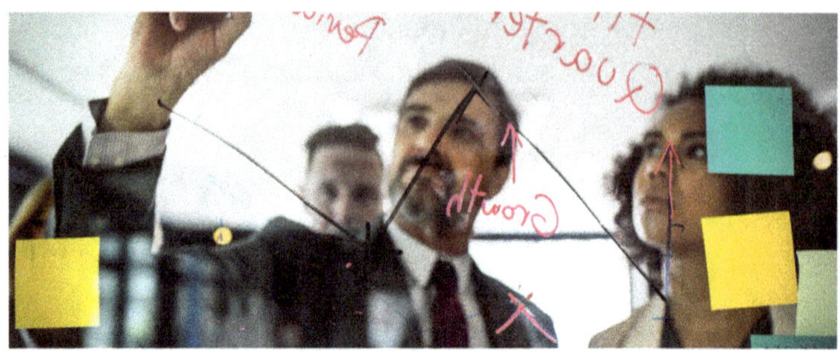

Conflict resolution models provide structured approaches for resolving conflicts peacefully and effectively. In this section, we introduce some well-established models and explain how they can be applied in practical terms to navigate difficult conversations and resolve conflicts.

A.   Thomas-Kilmann Conflict Mode Instrument (TKI):

The TKI is a widely recognized conflict resolution model that categorizes conflict-handling styles into five modes:

Competing | Collaborating | Compromising | Avoiding | Accommodating

In a corporate setting, a team was faced with a critical decision-making moment that required collaboration. The team members had diverse conflict-handling styles, and the leader wanted to ensure that everyone's perspective was considered.

a.   **Identifying Conflict Styles:** Learn to recognize your own and others' conflict-handling styles. Understand that individuals may have different default styles.

b.   **Choosing the Appropriate Mode:** Depending on the nature of the conflict and your goals, select the most appropriate mode from the TKI framework.

B. Interest-Based Relational Approach (IBRA):

The Interest-Based Relational Approach, often associated with principled negotiation, emphasizes the importance of focusing on interests, needs, and relationships rather than positions.

1. **Identifying Interests:** Encourage parties involved in the conflict to express their underlying interests and needs Actively listen to their concerns.

2. **Creating Value:** Seek opportunities to create value in the negotiation by identifying shared interests and collaborative solutions.

C. Practical Application of Conflict Models:

When applying conflict resolution models, ensure you follow a systematic process:

In a family setting, conflicts arose over the division of responsibilities. Different family members had varying expectations, leading to tension.

a. **Assess the Situation:** Evaluate the nature and context of the conflict, as well as the parties involved.

b. **Select the Model:** Choose the most appropriate conflict resolution model based on the specific circumstances.

c. **Communication:** Establish clear and open lines of communication between the parties involved.

d. **Interest Identification:** Encourage all parties to articulate their interests and concerns.

e. **Generate Options:** Collaboratively generate potential solutions that address the interests of all parties.

f. **Evaluate and Choose:** Assess the proposed solutions, consider their feasibility and impact, and choose the most suitable option.

g. **Agreement and Implementation:** Draft a formal agreement based on the chosen solution and ensure its successful implementation.

An assessment was conducted to understand each family member's perspective and expectations regarding responsibilities.

Clear and open lines of communication were established, allowing family members to express their concerns and viewpoints openly.

Through collaborative discussions, each family member articulated their interests and concerns regarding the division of responsibilities.

Family members worked together to generate potential solutions that addressed the interests of all parties involved.

Assessing the proposed solutions involved considering their feasibility and impact, leading to the selection of the most suitable option.

Drafting a formal agreement based on the chosen solution ensured its successful implementation, creating a shared plan for managing tasks.

D.   Mediation and Neutral Facilitation:

Consider involving a neutral mediator or facilitator to guide the conflict resolution process.

In a workplace conflict between employees, tensions were escalating, and a resolution seemed difficult to achieve through direct communication.

1. **Select a Skilled Mediator:** Choose a mediator or facilitator with expertise in conflict resolution and a neutral stance.

2. **Set Ground Rules:** Establish ground rules for the mediation or facilitation process to ensure a fair and constructive discussion.

The organization chose an experienced mediator with expertise in conflict resolution and a neutral stance to facilitate the resolution process.

Ground rules were established for the mediation process, ensuring a fair and constructive discussion. This structured and neutral environment allowed employees to address issues and reach a resolution.

Utilizing conflict resolution models empowers individuals to navigate difficult conversations effectively and reach mutually beneficial solutions. By understanding these models and applying them to specific conflict situations, you can foster collaboration, manage disputes, and promote peaceful resolutions in a structured manner.

Conflict Resolution Model Application – Now, let's put the conflict resolution models into action. Apply your knowledge to a hypothetical scenario:

Exercise: Choose a conflict scenario and apply the Thomas-Kilmann Conflict Mode Instrument (TKI) or the Interest-Based Relational Approach (IBRA). Select the most suitable conflict-handling style or approach and assess the outcomes. This practical exercise will deepen your understanding of conflict resolution models.

Ready to refine your skills further? Utilize the provided Conflict Resolution Model Application Worksheet (pg. 72⏎) in the consolidated section for a structured reflection on your experience. Outline the scenario, select your conflict resolution model, and evaluate the results.

Remember, mastery comes from practical application. Head to the consolidated section for more exercises and worksheets to enrich your communication and conflict resolution skills. Happy practicing!

CASE STUDIES AND SCENARIOS

Real-life case studies and scenarios serve as valuable tools to demonstrate the practical application of the concepts and strategies discussed in this guide. By examining these examples, you can gain insights into how to navigate difficult conversations effectively in diverse situations.

A. Workplace Conflict Resolution:

Imagine a scenario in a professional workplace where two team members, Alice and Bob, are involved in a heated dispute. Alice is upset about Bob not meeting project deadlines, while Bob feels overwhelmed and misunderstood. This scenario explores how the principles outlined in the guide can be applied to resolve their conflict and improve communication.

To address their conflict effectively, both Alice and Bob can take the following steps:

ENGAGE IN ACTIVE LISTENING:

Both Alice and Bob should actively listen to each other's concerns without interruptions. For example, Alice can say, "Bob, I want to understand why we missed those deadlines. Can you explain your perspective?" This shows that she is willing to listen and understand Bob's side.

MANAGE EMOTIONS:

They should recognize their own emotions and control their reactions. If Bob is feeling overwhelmed, he can say, "I'm sorry for not meeting the deadlines. I felt overwhelmed by the workload and deadlines. Let's discuss how we can address this."

APPLY PROBLEM-SOLVING TECHNIQUES:

Encourage them to work collaboratively to find solutions. They can brainstorm ways to meet deadlines, allocate tasks more efficiently, or request additional resources. For instance, "Let's brainstorm ideas on how we can meet our project deadlines together."

FOSTER A POSITIVE WORKING RELATIONSHIP:

It's essential to rebuild trust and foster a more positive working relationship. Alice can express her commitment to working together by saying, "I believe we can overcome these challenges and work better as a team. Let's put this behind us and focus on solutions."

B.   Family Dynamics and Disagreements:

Consider a family scenario where there are ongoing disagreements between siblings about managing their elderly parents' care. Each sibling has different opinions and concerns. This scenario demonstrates how cultural sensitivity, empathy, and problem-solving techniques can be applied to find common ground and make decisions that benefit everyone.

Family members can navigate the situation by:

EMPHASIZING CULTURAL SENSITIVITY:

Siblings should respect each other's cultural backgrounds and values. For example, if one sibling suggests a specific care tradition, others can acknowledge its importance even if it's different from their own.

PRACTICING EMPATHY AND UNDERSTANDING:

Each sibling should actively listen to the others' concerns and express empathy. For instance, "I understand that you're worried about our parents' well-being. I share the same concern, and I appreciate your perspective."

USING EFFECTIVE PROBLEM-SOLVING APPROACHES:

Siblings can collaborate to find solutions. They might use techniques such as setting up a family meeting to openly discuss their concerns, sharing responsibilities, or involving a professional mediator.

C.   Cross-Cultural Negotiation:

In a cross-cultural business negotiation scenario, two companies from different countries are attempting to form a partnership. They encounter challenges related to language barriers, varying negotiation styles, and misunderstandings. This scenario showcases the significance of cultural sensitivity and adapting communication to different personalities in a business context.

Successful negotiation and collaboration between the two companies can be achieved by:

UNDERSTANDING CULTURAL NUANCES:

Company representatives must educate themselves about each other's cultures to avoid misunderstandings. For instance, understanding how greetings, business etiquette, and hierarchy work in the other culture is essential.

RESPECTING DIVERSE COMMUNICATION STYLES:

Negotiators should adapt their communication styles to bridge language and stylistic gaps. Avoiding jargon, speaking slowly, and seeking clarification can facilitate better understanding.

BUILDING RAPPORT AND TRUST:

Developing personal connections and rapport with counterparts can help overcome cultural barriers. Socializing, sharing meals, and engaging in small talk can build trust, making negotiations smoother.

D. Customer Service Dilemma:

Imagine a customer service situation where a customer is dissatisfied with a product and contacts a customer service representative, Jane, to express their concerns. Jane, as the representative, needs to apply effective conflict resolution strategies, active listening, and empathy to address the customer's issues and retain their loyalty.

Jane can effectively manage the situation by:

ENGAGING IN ACTIVE LISTENING:

Jane should listen actively to the customer's concerns. She can paraphrase the customer's issues to show understanding. For example, "I hear that you've encountered problems with our product. I'm here to help."

APPLYING CONFLICT RESOLUTION STRATEGIES AND EMPATHY:

Jane should express empathy, showing that she values the customer's feedback. She can say, "I'm genuinely sorry for the inconvenience this has caused. Your feedback is important to us, and we want to resolve this."

OFFERING SOLUTIONS:

Jane can offer solutions or alternatives to address the customer's issues. This could include troubleshooting steps, replacement of the product, or offering discounts or incentives for their next purchase.

E.   Community Dispute Resolution:

In a community context, there is a dispute between neighbors regarding a property boundary issue. The dispute has escalated to the point of legal action. This scenario emphasizes the significance of mediation, neutrality, and following a structured conflict resolution model to reach a fair and mutually agreeable resolution.

A peaceful resolution can be achieved by:

INVOLVING A NEUTRAL MEDIATOR:

Both parties should agree to work with a neutral mediator who can facilitate a structured conversation. The mediator ensures that the dialogue remains constructive and fair.

ADHERING TO ESTABLISHED CONFLICT RESOLUTION MODELS:

Parties should follow a structured conflict resolution model such as the Interest-Based Relational Approach (IBRA). This model helps identify underlying interests and mutually agreeable solutions.

CONSIDERING INTERESTS OF BOTH PARTIES:

During the mediation, neighbors should focus on their shared interests, such as maintaining a peaceful living environment, rather than their positions. They can identify common goals for a peaceful resolution.

PRACTICE EXERCISES AND WORKSHEETS

Welcome to the consolidated section, a dedicated space crafted for your journey to mastery in effective communication and conflict resolution. Here, you'll discover a carefully curated collection of practice exercises and worksheets meticulously designed to reinforce the concepts discussed throughout this guide. These resources are more than tools— they are your companions on the path to honing essential skills.

To solidify your understanding and apply the strategies gleaned from this guide, immerse yourself in a range of practice exercises. These exercises target different facets of effective communication and conflict resolution, offering hands-on experiences that guide you in navigating difficult conversations successfully. These resources are not mere activities; they are designed to enhance your skills, providing a structured approach to your personal and professional development.

A.   Active Listening Exercise:

Engaging in active listening is a fundamental aspect of effective communication. Use this worksheet to guide your reflection and learning as you put active listening into practice. Jot down your observations, identify areas for improvement, and track your progress. The structured format will enhance your understanding and application of active listening principles.

Exercise: Listen to a podcast or engage in a conversation with a friend. As you listen, make a conscious effort to practice active listening. Summarize the main points, ask open-ended questions, and reflect on your experience.

Complete this exercise to apply the active listening principles discussed in the theory section of "Effective Communication Strategies" (pg. 13⧉). Then, return to this worksheet to document your observations and insights. This reflective process will deepen your active listening skills and contribute to your overall growth in effective communication.

ACTIVE LISTENING WORKSHEET

Date:_______________________

Name: **Listening Activity:**

INSTRUCTIONS:

In this exercise, you'll practice active listening during a conversation or while listening to a podcast or presentation. Active listening involves giving your full attention to the speaker and demonstrating that you are engaged and empathetic. Use this worksheet to jot down your observations, reflect on your listening skills, and identify areas for improvement.

Briefly describe the conversation or podcast you engaged in:

- ◉ Title/Topic: _________________________________
- ◉ Speaker(s): _________________________________
- ◉ Duration: _________________________________

ACTIVE LISTENING OBSERVATIONS:

1. **Give Your Full Attention:**

   - ◉ Describe how you ensured you were fully present during the conversation. Did you minimize distractions, put away electronic devices, or maintain eye contact?

2. **Use of Verbal Cues:**

   - ◉ List some verbal cues or responses you used to show the speaker that you were actively listening. For example, did you say "I understand," "I see," or nod your head?

3. **Paraphrasing and Reflecting:**

   - ◉ Share an instance where you paraphrased what the speaker said to ensure you understood correctly. How did this help the conversation?

4. **Ask Open-Ended Questions:**

   - ◉ Provide an example of an open-ended question you asked to encourage the speaker to share more. How did this contribute to the conversation?

____

____

____

REFLECTION:

- ◉ What did you find effective about your active listening skills during this activity?

- ◉ Were there any challenges or areas where you could improve your active listening? If so, how can you address these challenges in the future?

____

____

____

- List a few key takeaways from the conversation or podcast that you found valuable.

____

____

____

B. Emotional Self-Regulation Practice:

Engaging in emotional self-regulation is crucial for effective communication. Utilize this worksheet to guide your reflection and learning as you apply emotional self-regulation techniques. Document your emotional responses, evaluate the effectiveness of your chosen strategies, and monitor your progress. The structured format will enhance your understanding and application of emotional self-regulation principles.

 **Exercise:** Select a recent situation that triggered strong emotions. Practice deep breathing, mindfulness exercises, or relaxation techniques to manage your emotions and maintain a calm demeanor.

Use this exercise to apply emotional self-regulation techniques discussed in the theory section of "Managing Difficult Emotions" (pg. 17). Return to this worksheet afterward to document your observations and insights. This reflective process will deepen your emotional self-regulation skills and contribute to your overall growth in effective communication.

EMOTIONAL SELF-REGULATION WORKSHEET

Date:____________________

Name: **Triggering Situation:**

INSTRUCTIONS:

In this exercise, you will practice emotional self-regulation by reflecting on a recent situation that triggered strong emotions. Use this worksheet to track your emotional responses and the effectiveness of your self-regulation strategies.

TRIGGERING SITUATION:

Briefly describe the recent situation that triggered strong emotions:

- ◉ Situation Description: ____________________________
- ◉ Emotions Experienced: ____________________________

1. **Control Your Breathing:**

    - Describe the deep breathing or relaxation techniques you used to manage your emotions. How did these strategies affect your emotional state?

2. **Positive Self-Talk:**

    - Share examples of positive self-talk you engaged in to counter anxious or negative thoughts. How did this help you regain composure?

3. **Planning and Preparation:**

    - Explain how planning and preparing for the situation contributed to your emotional self-regulation. Did anticipating the situation boost your confidence?

4. **Accepting Imperfection:**

    - Reflect on whether you accepted the possibility of imperfection in the conversation. How did this acceptance influence your emotional state?

____

____

____

EFFECTIVENESS AND LEARNINGS:

- Rate the effectiveness of your emotional self-regulation strategies on a scale of 1 to 10, with 1 being not effective and 10 being highly effective.

- List any learnings or insights gained from this exercise. How can you apply these learnings to future situations that trigger strong emotions?

____

____

____

- Summarize the key takeaways from this exercise in terms of managing your emotions in challenging situations.

____

____

____

C. Problem-Solving Scenarios:

Mastering the art of problem-solving requires practical application. Use this worksheet to guide your reflection and learning as you engage in problem-solving scenarios. Collaborate with a partner or a group to identify issues, generate potential solutions, and make informed decisions. The structured format will enhance your understanding and application of problem-solving principles.

Exercise: Collaborate with a partner or a group to engage in problem-solving exercises that simulate real-life scenarios. Work together to identify issues, brainstorm potential solutions, and make informed decisions.

Complete this exercise to apply problem-solving principles from "Problem-Solving and Decision-Making" (pg. 29⬈) in a practical setting, and then use the Problem-Solving Scenarios Worksheet to outline scenarios, record potential solutions, and evaluate the decision-making process. This reflective process will contribute to your overall growth in effective communication and conflict resolution.

PROBLEM-SOLVING SCENARIOS WORKSHEET

Date:_________________

Name:

INSTRUCTIONS:

In this exercise, you will engage in problem-solving exercises that simulate real-life scenarios. Work with a partner or a group to collectively identify issues, generate solutions, and make informed decisions. Use this worksheet to outline the scenarios, record potential solutions, and evaluate the decision-making process.

- ◉ Describe the Scenario: _______________________________________
- ◉ Issue/Conflict to Solve: _______________________________________

SOLUTION OPTIONS:

1. Option 1: _______________________________________

2. Option 2: _______________________________________

3. Option 3: _______________________________________

SOLUTION EVALUATION:

- ◉ For each option, discuss the pros and cons. Consider the feasibility, impact, and potential consequences.

Option 1:

- ◉ Pros: _______________________________________
- ◉ Cons: _______________________________________

Option 2:

- ◉ Pros: _______________________________________
- ◉ Cons: _______________________________________

Option 3:

- ◉ Pros: _______________________________________
- ◉ Cons: _______________________________________

____

____

____

- After evaluating the options, make a decision on which solution to pursue.

____

____

____

- Summarize the key takeaways from these problem-solving scenarios in terms of the decision-making process and evaluating potential solutions.

____

____

____

D. Feedback Exchange Practice:

Refine your feedback exchange skills using the worksheet designed to structure your reflections and enhance your learning. Taking turns giving and receiving feedback is a valuable exercise in effective communication and conflict resolution. Utilize the structured format of the Feedback Exchange Worksheet to document key points, note areas for improvement, and track your progress.

Exercise: Pair up with a friend or colleague to engage in feedback exchange. Take turns giving and receiving feedback on a specific topic or situation, using the guidelines provided in this guide for constructive feedback.

After completing the exercise, use the Feedback Exchange Worksheet to structure your reflections. This reflective process will deepen your feedback exchange skills from "Giving and Receiving Feedback" (pg. 36⬀) and contribute to your overall growth in effective communication and conflict resolution.

FEEDBACK EXCHANGE WORKSHEET

Date:_____________________

Name:

INSTRUCTIONS:

In this exercise, you will pair up with a friend or colleague and take turns giving and receiving feedback on a specific topic or situation. Use this worksheet to structure your feedback conversations, document key points, and note areas for improvement.

FEEDBACK PROVIDER:

- ◉ Your Name: ________________________________

- ◉ Feedback Recipient's Name: ________________________

- ◉ Feedback Topic/Scenario: ____________________________

1. Offer constructive feedback to the recipient.

2. Focus on specific observations and examples.

3. Use "I" statements to express your feelings and perspective.

4. Be honest and respectful in your feedback.

5. Offer suggestions for improvement if relevant.

6. Encourage the recipient to ask questions or seek clarification.

FEEDBACK PROVIDER'S FEEDBACK:

- Describe the feedback you provided, including specific observations and examples.

____

____

____

RECIPIENT'S RESPONSE:

- How did the recipient react to the feedback? Did they ask questions or seek clarification?

____

____

____

INSTRUCTIONS FOR THE FEEDBACK RECIPIENT:

1. Listen actively to the feedback provided.

2. Ask questions or seek clarification if any points are unclear.

3. Reflect on the feedback and consider potential areas for improvement.

4. Express your appreciation for the feedback provided.

RECIPIENT'S SELF-REFLECTION:

- ◉ Reflect on the feedback received and how it made you feel.

____

____

____

RECIPIENT'S ACTION PLAN:

- ◉ Describe any actions or improvements you plan to make based on the feedback.

____

____

____

KEY TAKEAWAYS:

- ◉ Summarize the key takeaways from this feedback exchange experience in terms of communication and potential areas for improvement.

____

____

____

E. Cultural Sensitivity Reflection:

Enhance your cultural sensitivity through thoughtful reflection using this worksheet. Cultural nuances play a significant role in communication, and recognizing them is key to effective interaction. The Cultural Sensitivity Reflection Worksheet provides a structured format to document your reflections, recognize cultural differences, and identify opportunities for improvement.

Exercise: Reflect on a recent interaction with someone from a different cultural background. Consider the cultural nuances and communication styles that were at play during the conversation.

Utilize the Cultural Sensitivity Reflection Worksheet to assist you in documenting your reflections. This reflective process will deepen your cultural sensitivity as discussed in "Cultural Sensitivity and Diversity" (pg. 40⬀) and contribute to your overall growth in effective communication and conflict resolution.

CULTURAL SENSITIVITY REFLECTION WORKSHEET

Date:_________________

Name:

INSTRUCTIONS:

In this exercise, you will reflect on a recent interaction with someone from a different cultural background. Consider the cultural nuances and communication styles that were at play during the conversation. Use this worksheet to document your reflections, recognize cultural differences, and identify opportunities for improvement.

INTERACTION DETAILS:

- ◉ Date of Interaction: _____________
- ◉ Participants in the Interaction: _____________________________
- ◉ Cultural Background of the Other Person: ____________________________

- Describe the context and purpose of the interaction with the person from a different cultural background.

____

____

____

- Reflect on your observations during the interaction. What cultural nuances or communication styles did you notice? Were there any challenges or misunderstandings?

____

____

____

- Consider your own communication style during the interaction. Did you adapt your approach to accommodate the cultural differences? If so, how?

____

____

____

CULTURAL DIFFERENCES AND INSIGHTS:

- List any specific cultural differences you recognized during the interaction (e.g., communication style, body language, greetings, etc.).

____

____

____

- ◉ Reflect on how these cultural differences may have influenced the dynamics of the conversation. Did they impact the effectiveness of the communication?

____

____

____

OPPORTUNITIES FOR IMPROVEMENT:

- ◉ Identify opportunities for improvement in future interactions with individuals from diverse cultural backgrounds.

____

____

____

- ◉ Consider how you can enhance your cultural sensitivity and adaptability in similar situations.

____

____

____

KEY TAKEAWAYS:

- ◉ Summarize the key takeaways from this cultural sensitivity reflection exercise and note how they can help you navigate cross-cultural conversations more effectively in the future.

____

____

____

F. Conflict Resolution Model Application:

Deepen your understanding of "Conflict Resolution Models" (pg. 44⚓) by applying them to real-world scenarios. The Conflict Resolution Model Application Worksheet guides you through the process of outlining a scenario, selecting the appropriate conflict resolution model, and assessing the outcomes.

Exercise: Apply the Thomas-Kilmann Conflict Mode Instrument (TKI) or the Interest-Based Relational Approach (IBRA) to a hypothetical conflict scenario. Choose the most suitable conflict-handling style or approach and assess the results.

Use the Conflict Resolution Model Application Worksheet to structure your reflection. This hands-on exercise will enhance your ability to navigate conflicts effectively and collaboratively.

CONFLICT RESOLUTION MODEL APPLICATION WORKSHEET

Date:_____________________

Name:

INSTRUCTIONS:

In this exercise, you will apply the Thomas-Kilmann Conflict Mode Instrument (TKI) or the Interest-Based Relational Approach (IBRA) to a hypothetical conflict scenario. Choose the most suitable conflict-handling style or approach and evaluate the results. Use this worksheet to outline the scenario, select your conflict resolution model, and assess the outcomes.

CONFLICT SCENARIO DETAILS:

- ◉ Date of Scenario: _____________________
- ◉ Description of the Conflict Scenario: _____________________

Choose either the Thomas-Kilmann Conflict Mode Instrument (TKI) or the Interest-Based Relational Approach (IBRA) as your conflict resolution model.

SELECTED CONFLICT RESOLUTION MODEL:

[   ] TKI

[   ] IBRA

____

____

____

APPLICATION OF THE CONFLICT RESOLUTION MODEL:

1. **Identify the parties involved in the conflict and their roles:**

   ◉ Party 1:
     • Role:

   ◉ Party 2:
     • Role:

2. **Analyze the nature of the conflict:**

   ◉ Describe the primary issues or concerns leading to the conflict.

3. **Apply the chosen conflict resolution model:**

   ◉ Explain how you would apply the model to address the conflict scenario. What steps or strategies would you follow?

4. **Assess the outcomes:**

   ◉ Consider the potential results of using the chosen model. How would it impact the parties involved and the resolution of the conflict?

5. **Reflect on the effectiveness of the chosen model:**

   ◉ Evaluate whether the chosen model is suitable for this scenario. What worked well, and what challenges did you encounter?

6. **Consider alternative approaches:**

- Are there other conflict resolution models that might have been more effective in this scenario?

7. **Key Takeaways:**

- Summarize the key takeaways from this conflict resolution model application exercise. Note any insights that can help you handle real-life conflicts more effectively.

____

____

____

These practice exercises and worksheets are designed to be versatile and adaptable to different situations. They offer you the opportunity to actively practice and reinforce the skills and strategies discussed in the guide, ensuring that you can confidently navigate difficult conversations with effectiveness and empathy.

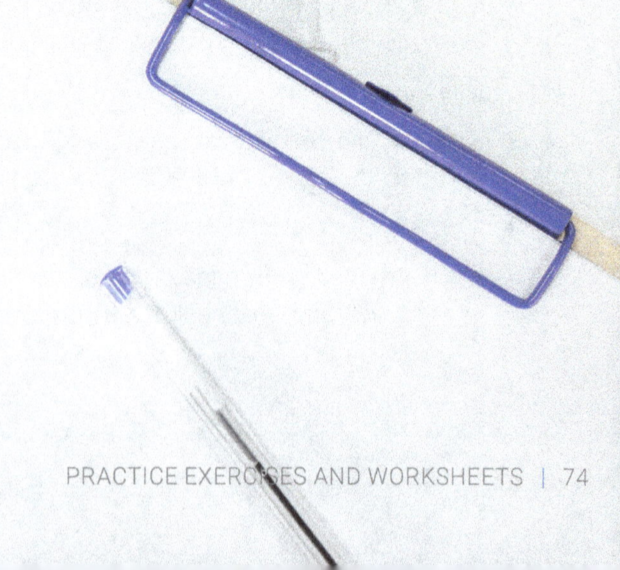

FINAL THOUGHTS AND RECAP

As we conclude this guide on "Difficult Conversation Guide: Navigating Challenging Conversations with Empathy, Skill, and Effectiveness," we want to revisit the essential principles and strategies discussed throughout the guide. By summarizing key takeaways and providing a motivational message, we aim to empower you to apply what you've learned in your own difficult conversations and interactions.

In your journey to becoming a more effective communicator and conflict resolver, consider the following key takeaways from this guide:

1. **Cultivate an Open Mindset:** Approach difficult conversations with an open and non-judgmental mindset to create a safe and trusting space for dialogue.

2. **Acknowledge and Manage Emotions:** Recognize the impact of emotions on conversations and learn techniques to manage emotions constructively.

3. **Clarify Your Intentions:** Set clear, honest, and positive intentions for each conversation, focusing on mutual understanding rather than winning.

4. **Develop Emotional Intelligence:** Practice self-awareness, self-regulation, empathy, and social skills to enhance your emotional intelligence.

5. **Use SMART Goals:** Employ Specific, Measurable, Achievable, Relevant, and Time-bound goals for conversations to provide structure and clarity.

6. **Explore Effective Communication Strategies:** Delve into techniques such as active listening, non-verbal communication, and tone of voice to enhance your communication skills.

7. **Manage Difficult Emotions:** Learn to manage specific emotions commonly encountered in difficult conversations, such as anger, defensiveness, and anxiety.

8. **Handle Resistance and Opposition:** Discover techniques for defusing tension and fostering a collaborative atmosphere when faced with resistance or defensiveness.

9. **Build Rapport and Trust:** Understand the importance of establishing, maintaining, and rebuilding trust during challenging dialogues.

10. **Effective Problem-Solving:** Embrace a structured approach to jointly identify issues, generate solutions, and make informed decisions in the context of difficult conversations.

11. **Adapt to Different Personalities:** Tailor your communication style to engage effectively with various personality types, recognizing that one size does not fit all.

12. **Give and Receive Feedback:** Master the art of offering constructive feedback and accepting feedback with an open mind during challenging conversations.

13. **Embrace Cultural Sensitivity:** Recognize the significance of cultural sensitivity and diversity in communication, learning how to navigate conversations with people from diverse backgrounds.

14. **Utilize Conflict Resolution Models:** Implement well-established conflict resolution models like the Thomas-Kilmann Conflict Mode Instrument (TKI) and the Interest-Based Relational Approach in practical terms to resolve conflicts peacefully and effectively.

15. **Apply Concepts Through Case Studies:** Learn to apply the principles and strategies through real-life case studies and scenarios that demonstrate the practical application in diverse situations.

16. **Reinforce Learning with Practice Exercises:** Strengthen your skills through a range of practice exercises and worksheets tailored to different aspects of effective communication and conflict resolution.

Your journey doesn't end here; it continues in your daily interactions, conversations, and relationships. To keep building on what you've learned:

1. **Practice, Practice, Practice:** The more you practice the strategies and techniques covered in this guide, the more proficient you will become. Challenge yourself with different scenarios and diverse individuals to hone your skills.

2. **Self-Reflection:** Regularly take a moment to reflect on your communication experiences. Analyze what went well and identify areas for improvement. Self-awareness is key to growth.

3. **Seek Support:** Don't hesitate to seek support and guidance from mentors, coaches, or friends who can provide valuable feedback and insights.

4. **Stay Informed:** Stay current with the latest developments in communication and conflict resolution. The field is continually evolving, and staying informed can enhance your effectiveness.

5. **Share Your Knowledge:** Consider sharing the knowledge and skills you've gained with others. By helping others navigate difficult conversations, you reinforce your own learning.

6. **Celebrate Progress:** Celebrate your successes, no matter how small they may seem. Every positive interaction and resolution is a step forward.

Remember that the journey to becoming an effective communicator is ongoing. We encourage you to apply the principles and strategies outlined in this guide to your daily life, both personally and professionally. By doing so, you can make a significant difference in how you navigate difficult conversations, build understanding, and foster positive outcomes. You have the power to create more empathetic and effective communication in your world.

▮ A MOTIVATIONAL MESSAGE:

As we reach the conclusion of this guide on "Difficult Conversation Guide: Navigating Challenging Conversations with Empathy, Skill, and Effectiveness," let's encapsulate the essence of our journey.

> *"Beyond Skill, Your Success in Communication Depends on Your Mindset and Intent!"*

This philosophy has been our beacon throughout, emphasizing that true mastery in communication extends beyond mere skills. It's about cultivating the right mindset and intention.

Remember the realizations you have had as you went through this guide that has been articulated from the crucible of real-life conversations and shaped by diverse global perspectives. Derived from interactions worldwide, coaching conversations with senior executives, and the nuanced insights of a Mindset Coach and Design Thinking Mentor, it captures lessons drawn from over 15 years of collaboration in multicultural teams and the resilience forged in navigating the challenges of failed ventures.

As you move forward, equipped with advanced strategies, psychological insights, and practical exercises, carry with you the understanding that every difficult conversation is an opportunity for growth. Apply the principles with empathy, authenticity, and a genuine connection. Be the catalyst for positive change, the bridge to understanding, and the source of empathetic communication.

In the words of our guiding quote,

....

*"Self-realization is the
strongest advice."*

Let this self-awareness be your guiding light in navigating future conversations. With dedication and the principles outlined in this guide, you have the potential to master even the most challenging interactions.

Thank you for joining us on this transformative journey. May your communication be enriched, your relationships strengthened, and your impact resonant in every conversation.

****

Difficult Conversation Preparation CHECKLIST

Use this checklist to ensure you're fully prepared for your next difficult conversation.

By following these steps, you can enhance your confidence and effectiveness in navigating challenging dialogues.

1. PREPARE YOUR MINDSET

- Cultivate an open and non-judgmental mindset.
- Acknowledge your emotions and biases.
- Understand the impact of emotions on conversations.
- Learn techniques to manage emotions.
- Create a conducive atmosphere by managing your emotions effectively.

2. DEFINE YOUR PURPOSE

- Clarify your intentions and desired outcomes.
- Ensure your intentions are clear, honest, and aligned with a positive outcome.
- Set specific, measurable, achievable, relevant, and time-bound (SMART) goals for the conversation.

3. EFFECTIVE COMMUNICATION STRATEGIES

- Familiarize yourself with active listening techniques.
- Practice non-verbal communication skills.
- Consider your tone of voice and its impact.

4. MANAGING DIFFICULT EMOTIONS

- Identify potential emotional triggers.
- Develop strategies for managing emotions constructively.
- Plan how to stay calm and composed, even in the face of strong emotions.

5. DEALING WITH RESISTANCE AND OPPOSITION

- Prepare for potential resistance or defensiveness from the other party.
- Have techniques ready to defuse tension and foster a collaborative atmosphere.

6. BUILDING RAPPORT AND TRUST

- Plan how to establish, maintain, or rebuild trust during the conversation.
- Consider practical advice for creating a trusting environment.

7. EFFECTIVE PROBLEM-SOLVING AND DECISION-MAKING

- Familiarize yourself with problem-solving frameworks.
- Plan how to jointly identify issues, generate solutions, and make informed decisions.

8. HANDLING DIFFERENT PERSONALITIES

- Reflect on the personalities involved in the conversation.
- Consider how to adapt your communication style to engage effectively with different personality types.

9. GIVING AND RECEIVING FEEDBACK

- Prepare to offer constructive feedback.
- Plan how to accept feedback with an open mind.

10. CULTURAL SENSITIVITY AND DIVERSITY

- Reflect on potential cultural differences.
- Plan strategies for navigating conversations with people from diverse backgrounds.

11. CONFLICT RESOLUTION MODELS

- Familiarize yourself with conflict resolution models.
- Plan how to apply these models in practical terms to resolve conflicts effectively.

12. CASE STUDIES AND SCENARIOS

- Review case studies or scenarios for practical application.

13. PRACTICE EXERCISES AND WORKSHEETS

- Complete additional practice exercises and worksheets to reinforce your learning.

14. FINAL THOUGHTS AND RECAP

- Reflect on the key takeaways from the guide.
- Plan your next steps for applying what you've learned.

Remember, preparation is key to success in difficult conversations. This checklist can help you systematically prepare for your challenging dialogues and contribute to positive outcomes.

< References >

1. Fisher, R., Ury, W., & Patton, B. (2011). "Getting to Yes: Negotiating Agreement Without Giving In." Penguin Books.

2. Stone, D., Patton, B., & Heen, S. (1999). "Difficult Conversations: How to Discuss What Matters Most." Penguin Books.

3. Goleman, D. (1996). "Emotional Intelligence: Why It Can Matter More Than IQ." Bantam Books.

4. Kilmann, R. H., & Thomas, K. W. (1975). "The Thomas-Kilmann Conflict Mode Instrument." Tuxedo, NY: Xicom, Inc.

5. Pruitt, D. G., & Carnevale, P. J. (2003). "Negotiation in Social Conflict." Open Road Media.

6. Tannen, D. (2001). "You Just Don't Understand: Women and Men in Conversation." Harper Paperbacks.

7. Patterson, K., Grenny, J., McMillan, R., & Switzler, A. (2011). "Crucial Conversations: Tools for Talking When Stakes Are High." McGraw-Hill Education.

8. Triandis, H. C. (1994). "Culture and Social Behavior." McGraw-Hill.

9. Shapiro, D. L., & Sheppard, B. H. (2019). "Negotiating the Nonnegotiable: How to Resolve Your Most Emotionally Charged Conflicts." Penguin.

10. Collins, J. (2001). "Good to Great: Why Some Companies Make the Leap... and Others Don't." HarperBusiness.

Additional Resources for Further Exploration:

In your journey to master the art of navigating difficult conversations, you may want to explore additional resources to further enhance your knowledge and skills. Here are some recommended books, articles, and courses that can help you delve deeper into this subject:

Books:

1. "Crucial Conversations: Tools for Talking When Stakes Are High" by Al Switzler, Joseph Grenny, and Ron McMillan.
2. "Difficult Conversations: How to Discuss What Matters Most" by Douglas Stone, Bruce Patton, and Sheila Heen.
3. "Nonviolent Communication: A Language of Life" by Marshall B. Rosenberg.
4. "Emotional Intelligence: Why It Can Matter More Than IQ" by Daniel Goleman.

Online Courses:

1. Coursera offers courses on "Conflict Resolution" and "Negotiation, Leadership, and Influence" that can further develop your skills.
2. LinkedIn Learning provides courses such as "Difficult Conversations" and "Managing Conflict."

Articles:

1. Harvard Business Review offers various articles on communication, conflict resolution, and difficult conversations.
2. Explore psychology and communication journals for scholarly articles on the topic.

Remember that these resources serve as valuable supplements to the knowledge you gain from this guide. Feel free to explore them as you continue your journey towards becoming an effective communicator and conflict resolver.

Dedicated FAQ Section:

Below are answers to some frequently asked questions about handling difficult conversations:

Q1: **How do I approach a difficult conversation when emotions are running high?**

When emotions are intense, it's crucial to remain calm and composed. Here are steps to consider:

- ✓ **Take a moment to breathe and give yourself time to collect your thoughts.** For example, if a colleague confronts you with an angry tone about a project delay, you can say, "I can see you're upset. Let's discuss this, but can we take a short break to gather our thoughts?"

- ✓ **Acknowledge your emotions.** Recognize what you're feeling and why. For instance, if you're discussing household responsibilities with your partner and you feel overwhelmed, you can say, "I'm feeling overwhelmed because I think we should share these responsibilities more evenly."

- ✓ **Encourage the other person to share their feelings.** Active listening is a powerful tool. Let them express themselves and validate their emotions. If a friend is upset with you for not attending an event, you can say, "I understand you're upset. I'd like to hear your perspective and explain why I couldn't make it."

- ✓ **Practice empathy.** Try to understand the other person's perspective and feelings. This can help defuse tension and open the door to a more constructive conversation. For instance, if your team member is frustrated with a new project, you can say, "I understand you're frustrated. Can you help me understand what's been challenging for you?"

Q2: **What if the other person becomes defensive during a conversation?**

If someone becomes defensive, it's essential to handle the situation with care and tact.

- ✓ **Avoid blame or accusations.** Instead of saying, "You're always late with your reports," you can rephrase it as, "I've noticed that the reports have been arriving later than expected."

- ☑ **Stay open-minded.** For instance, if the other person expresses frustration, you can respond with, "I understand that you're frustrated, and I want to hear your thoughts."

- ☑ **Use empathetic statements.** If they say, "I can't believe you're bringing this up again," you can respond with, "I know this topic has come up before, and I appreciate your patience."

- ☑ **Ask clarifying questions.** For example, you can ask, "Could you help me understand what led to this situation?"

- ☑ **Emphasize understanding their perspective.** You can say, "I genuinely want to understand where you're coming from in this matter."

Q3: How do I rebuild trust after a difficult conversation has strained a relationship?

Rebuilding trust takes time and effort. Here's how to begin the process:

- ☑ **Acknowledge any mistakes:** If your actions or words played a part in straining the relationship, it's important to admit to them. For example, if you had a disagreement with a friend over a misunderstanding, you can say, "I realize that I should have communicated more clearly, and I'm sorry for the confusion."

- ☑ **Apologize if necessary:** In cases where an apology is warranted, ensure it's sincere and specific. If you've unintentionally hurt someone's feelings during a conversation, apologize by saying, "I'm sorry for my words; they were insensitive, and I didn't mean to hurt you."

- ☑ **Demonstrate consistent behavior aligned with your words:** Your actions should match your promises and intentions. If you've committed to improving a situation, such as teamwork in your department, ensure your behavior reflects this commitment.

- ☑ **Open and honest communication:** Keep the lines of communication open. Share your thoughts and feelings, and encourage the other person to do the same. If you're mending a friendship, you can say, "I value our friendship and want to rebuild trust. How can we move forward together?"

 Can cultural differences complicate difficult conversations?

Cultural differences can indeed impact communication, but they don't have to be barriers. Here's how to navigate conversations effectively:

- ✓ **Begin by acknowledging and respecting diverse cultural backgrounds and communication styles.** For example, if you're working with colleagues from different countries, it's essential to recognize that their communication norms may vary.

- ✓ **Adapt your approach to the other person's cultural preferences, showing sensitivity to their unique background.** In a cross-cultural negotiation, consider how the negotiation style may differ based on cultural norms.

- ✓ **Seek to understand their perspective and how it may be influenced by their cultural norms and values.** For instance, someone from a collectivist culture may prioritize the group's harmony, while an individualist may focus on personal goals.

- ✓ **Embrace open dialogue and a willingness to learn from each other.** Engage in conversations that bridge cultural gaps and promote understanding.

Q5: **What's the best way to give constructive feedback during a challenging conversation?**

When giving feedback during a difficult conversation, these tips can be helpful:

- ✓ **Use "I" statements to express your perspective without sounding confrontational.** For instance, instead of saying, "You're always late, and it's disrespectful," you can say, "I've noticed that there have been instances where our meetings started later than planned, and it's been challenging for me."

- ✓ **Focus on specific behaviors, not personal attributes.** It's essential to address actions and behaviors, not make judgments about the person. For example, instead of saying, "You're disorganized," you can say, "I've noticed that our last project had some disorganization in the file structure."

- ✓ **Ensure the feedback is clear, specific, and solution-oriented.** Provide concrete examples and suggest potential solutions. For instance, "During our last team meeting, when we discussed the project timeline, your contributions were not clear, which made it challenging for the team to understand. To improve, maybe we can start by outlining your points before discussing them."

Q6: What should I do if the other person refuses to engage in the conversation or is unresponsive?

When someone you're trying to have a difficult conversation with is unresponsive or refuses to engage, here are some steps to consider:

- ✓ **Understand Their Reasons:** Try to understand why they might be unresponsive. It could be due to emotional overwhelm, fear, or a need for space. Avoid making assumptions and be empathetic.

- ✓ **Offer Space and Time:** Respect their need for space and time to process their thoughts and emotions. Let them know that you're open to talking when they feel ready.

- ✓ **Express Willingness:** Communicate your willingness to have the conversation in the future. Assure them that you value their perspective and that you're available when they decide to engage.

- ✓ **Avoid Pressure:** Avoid putting pressure on them or making them feel obligated to engage. Let it be a voluntary choice on their part.

- ✓ **Stay Patient:** Patience is essential in such situations. Give them the time they need, and don't rush the conversation.

Remember that forcing a conversation when someone is unresponsive can be counterproductive. It's often more effective to allow them to come to the discussion willingly when they feel ready.

Example: Imagine you're trying to discuss a sensitive work-related issue with a colleague who seems unresponsive during the conversation. Instead of pushing them to respond, you might say, "I can see that this is a challenging topic, and I want to give you some time to gather your thoughts. When you're ready to continue the conversation, please let me know. I value your input." This approach allows the person to regain composure and rejoin the discussion at their own pace.

Q7:   How can I ensure confidentiality during sensitive discussions?

When it comes to maintaining confidentiality in sensitive discussions, here are some steps to follow:

- ☑ **Set Ground Rules:** Establish clear ground rules at the beginning of the conversation regarding the confidentiality of the information shared. This sets the expectation that what is discussed will remain private.

- ☑ **Assure Privacy:** Reassure the other person that their information will be kept private. Emphasize the importance of trust and your commitment to safeguarding their confidentiality.

- ☑ **Limited Sharing:** Make it clear that information will only be shared with relevant parties if necessary. Ensure that any disclosure is within the agreed-upon boundaries.

- ☑ **Respect Their Concerns:** Encourage the other person to express any concerns they may have about confidentiality. Address their worries and reassure them.

- ☑ **Document Agreements:** If appropriate, document any confidentiality agreements to have a record of what was discussed and agreed upon.

Example: Let's say you need to discuss a sensitive HR matter with an employee. You could start the conversation by saying, "I want to assure you that our discussion will be confidential. What we talk about here will not be shared with anyone else unless it's necessary for resolving the issue, and we'll discuss and agree on that together." This approach establishes trust and clarifies the boundaries of confidentiality.

Q8:   What if I make a mistake during a difficult conversation?

Making a mistake during a challenging conversation is a common concern. Here's how to address it effectively:

- ☑ **Acknowledge the Mistake:** When you realize you've made a mistake, don't ignore it or try to cover it up. Acknowledge the error promptly.

- ☑ **Take Responsibility:** Taking responsibility for your mistake is crucial. Own up to your part in the misstep and avoid shifting blame onto others.

- ✓ **Apologize If Needed:** Depending on the situation and the impact of your mistake, offer a sincere apology if it's appropriate. A well-phrased apology can go a long way in rebuilding trust.

- ✓ **Use It as a Learning Opportunity:** View your mistake as a chance for personal growth. Reflect on what led to the error and how you can improve your communication skills in the future.

Q9: How can I prevent difficult conversations from escalating into arguments?

Preventing a difficult conversation from turning into an argument is essential for a productive discussion. Here are some steps to help you maintain a constructive dialogue:

- ✓ **Maintain a Calm Tone:** Speak calmly and avoid raising your voice, even if the conversation becomes heated. A calm tone can help de-escalate the situation.

- ✓ **Practice Active Listening:** Actively listen to the other person without interrupting. Make an effort to understand their perspective, and acknowledge their feelings.

- ✓ **Empathize:** Show empathy by validating their emotions and concerns. This can help create a more supportive atmosphere.

- ✓ **Consider Taking a Short Break:** If you notice the conversation is escalating and becoming unproductive, suggest taking a short break. This break can give both parties time to cool off and collect their thoughts.

Q10:   Are there situations where it's better to avoid or delay a difficult conversation?

Recognizing when it's appropriate to avoid or delay a challenging discussion is an important aspect of effective communication. Here are some situations in which delaying the conversation is advisable:

- ✓ **Extremely High Emotions:** When emotions are running extremely high, it's often best to delay the conversation. Emotional intensity can make it challenging to have a productive dialogue. Wait until everyone involved is calmer and can approach the discussion more rationally.

- ✓ **Lack of Preparation:** If you're not adequately prepared for the conversation, it's better to postpone it. Preparation includes understanding the issue, knowing your goals, and having a clear plan for the discussion. Being unprepared can lead to misunderstandings and unproductive outcomes.

 How can I address disagreements with family members without causing long-lasting rifts in our relationships?

Resolving disagreements within a family without causing long-lasting rifts requires a thoughtful and empathetic approach. Here are some steps to consider:

- ✓ **Open Communication:** Encourage open and honest communication within the family. Create an environment where everyone feels comfortable expressing their thoughts and feelings. Acknowledge that disagreements are a natural part of any relationship.

- ✓ **Empathy:** Practice empathy by trying to understand each family member's perspective. Empathizing with their feelings and viewpoints can help build a sense of connection, even during disagreements.

- ✓ **Compromise:** Strive for compromise and finding common ground. Understand that not every issue has a single solution, and sometimes you may need to meet in the middle. This demonstrates your willingness to work together.

Example: Suppose you and your sibling have different opinions on a family matter, such as how to care for an aging parent. Instead of allowing this disagreement to escalate into a rift, you could say, "I understand that we have different views on this, and it's essential that we both express our concerns. Let's try to find a solution that respects both of our perspectives. Maybe we can explore various options, like in-home care or assisted living, and weigh the pros and cons of each together." This approach keeps the lines of communication open and seeks a compromise that considers both viewpoints.

Q12: **What if a difficult conversation reveals deeply rooted family issues or unresolved conflicts from the past?**

If a challenging conversation reveals long-standing family issues or unresolved conflicts from the past, it's important to address these matters thoughtfully. Here's how to approach it:

- ✓ **Seek Professional Help:** Consider involving a family therapist or counselor who specializes in resolving family conflicts. They have the expertise to guide your family through these complex issues and provide a safe space for everyone to express their feelings.

- ☑ **Honest Discussion:** Encourage open and honest discussions within your family. Sometimes, acknowledging past conflicts and their impact is the first step towards healing. Create a non-judgmental environment where each family member can speak their truth.

- ☑ **Focus on Resolution:** The goal should be to find resolutions and reach a point of closure on these past issues. A therapist can provide strategies and exercises to help your family work through these challenges.

Example: Let's say you and your sibling are discussing a recent family dispute about an inheritance, and it triggers memories of a past family conflict. Instead of avoiding these issues, you might consider saying, "It seems like this discussion is bringing up unresolved conflicts from our past. We could benefit from professional guidance in working through these issues and finding a resolution that brings peace to our family. How do you feel about involving a family counselor to help us navigate this?" By suggesting professional help, you open the door to addressing deep-rooted family problems constructively.

Q13: **How do I navigate conversations with friends or loved ones about sensitive topics, such as addiction or mental health concerns?**

Conversations about sensitive topics like addiction or mental health concerns require a delicate approach. Here's how to navigate them effectively:

- ☑ **Express Concern:** Begin the conversation by expressing your genuine concern for their well-being. Let them know you care and are there to support them.

- ☑ **Choose the Right Time and Place:** Find a comfortable and private setting to have this discussion. It's important that both you and your loved one feel at ease during the conversation.

- ☑ **Listen Actively:** Practice active listening, allowing them to share their thoughts and feelings. Avoid judgment, and give them your full attention.

- ☑ **Encourage Professional Help:** If the situation warrants it, gently encourage them to seek professional assistance. Mention that professionals have the expertise to provide the right guidance and support.

- ☑ **Offer Support:** Reiterate your support and willingness to assist them in finding the help they need. Let them know they don't have to face these challenges alone.

Example: If you're concerned about a friend's alcohol use, you could say, "I've noticed that you've been drinking more frequently, and it's been affecting your well-being. I care about you and want to support you. Have you considered speaking to a therapist or counselor who can provide guidance on how to manage this situation effectively?" This approach combines your genuine concern with a practical solution, promoting a productive conversation about a sensitive topic.

Q14: **What should I do if a loved one is in denial or refuses to acknowledge their behavior as problematic during a conversation?**

When a loved one is in denial or unwilling to admit their behavior is problematic, it can be a challenging situation to address. Here's how to navigate it effectively:

- ☑ **Provide Evidence:** During the conversation, gently provide evidence of their behavior and its impact. Use specific examples and facts rather than general statements.

- ☑ **Stay Patient:** Understand that it may take time for them to come to terms with their behavior. Be patient and allow them space to process the information.

- ☑ **Offer Support:** Let them know that you are there to support them and that you care about their well-being. Reiterate that your intention is to help rather than judge.

- ☑ **Be Persistent but Gentle:** While it's important to be persistent in your approach, avoid pushing too hard, as it might cause resistance. Encourage open communication and express your willingness to discuss the issue further.

Q15: **How can I balance the need for personal boundaries with the desire for open communication in personal relationships?**

Balancing personal boundaries with open communication in personal relationships is crucial for healthy interactions. Here's how to strike that balance effectively:

- ✓ **Establish Clear Boundaries:** Start by defining your personal boundaries. Understand what you're comfortable with and what you're not. Be specific and clear about your limits.

- ✓ **Communicate Your Boundaries:** Once you've established your boundaries, communicate them to your loved ones. Express your needs and limitations respectfully and clearly.

- ✓ **Mutual Respect:** Emphasize the importance of mutual respect in your relationships. Let your loved ones know that respecting your boundaries is a way of showing care and consideration.

- ✓ **Open Communication:** Encourage open communication about boundaries. Ensure that your loved ones feel comfortable discussing their boundaries with you as well.

- ✓ **Flexibility and Adaptation:** While boundaries are important, be willing to adapt and be flexible when needed. Sometimes, situations may require a temporary adjustment of boundaries for the sake of understanding and compromise.

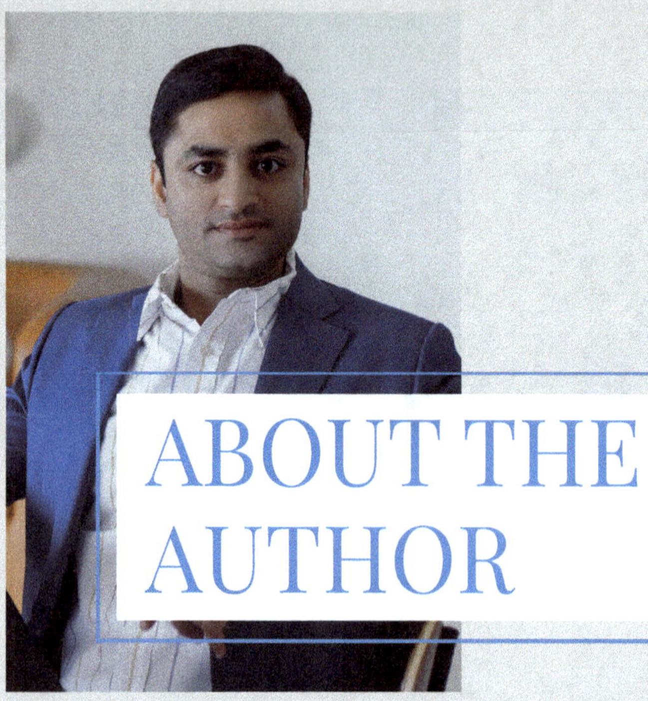

ABOUT THE AUTHOR

Journey alongside Rakesh Lazar, affectionately known as Coach Lazar, a seasoned Thinking Partner and Mindset Coach specializing in Communication Confidence.

As Rakesh elegantly puts it,

·········

"Self-realization is the strongest advice,"

drawing from personal experiences of success and failures. With a unique approach, he advocates for self-realization over advice, facilitating profound insights through coaching conversations that lead to sustainable and transformative changes.

With over 13 years of living in South Korea, Rakesh, an Indian married to a Russian, immerses himself in the kaleidoscope of human interactions across diverse cultures. As a Thinking Partner and Design Thinking Mentor, Rakesh has accumulated a profound perspective on the transformative power of communication.

A key organizer of TEDx and international events, Rakesh has played a pivotal role in shaping powerful and impactful deliveries as a stage host and speaker auditioner. With over 100 captivating talks and keynotes on human potential and positive psychology, Rakesh has keenly felt the transformative impact of effective communication.

Philosophizing that communication transcends mere skill, he advocates that mindset and intent shape words, guiding individuals authentically through any conversation. The guiding principle,

"Beyond Skill, Your Success in Communication Depends on Your Mindset and Intent"

underlines his belief that true communication mastery extends beyond skills alone. Coach Lazar is on a mission to help frustrated executives cultivate communication confidence, elevating their leadership influence and performance.

Fueling Rakesh's passion is the art of fine-tuning communication, personally facilitating over 380 individuals to achieve personal and professional success. Coaching outcomes include enhanced leadership influence, effective collaboration, improved public speaking skills, empowering others, and managing difficult conversations and conflicts.

As you conclude this guide, Rakesh invites you to carry the insights gained, applying them with empathy, authenticity, and a genuine connection.

Get ready to navigate future conversations with dedication, armed with the potential to master even the most challenging interactions.

Each One of Us Is Unique. An Exclusive DNA Composition!

Just as your fingerprints and the iris in your eye are one of a kind, so are your thoughts and emotions. There has never been anyone like 'you' before, and there never will be. ***It's all about 'you'!***

WHAT You Are? = Unique DNA

WHO You Are? = Key to Unlocking the Uniqueness.

We often look outside for standards, benchmarks, and social validation, unintentionally tarnishing our unique possibilities. What if you could awaken the best possibilities in you? Who would you become? What positive difference would that bring to you, your family, your team, and your dreams?

There are certain parts of yourself that require a mirror to See.

Self-Awareness Awakened Through a Deep Conversation Is the Method to The Magic.

That Is What It Would Mean to Get on Your Coaching Journey with Me as Your Thinking Partner, Your Talking Mirror.

Connect with Coach Lazar

COMMUNICATION CONFIDENCE COACHING

I Help Frustrated Executives with Cultivating Communication Confidence to Elevate Their Leadership Influence and Performance.

"Beyond Skill, Your Success in Communication Depends on Your Mindset and Intent"

Your words are the articulation of your thought process and confidence.

Rakesh.Lazar@gmail.com

PERSONAL MASTERY COACHING

I Guide You Through Exploring, Harnessing, And Leveraging Your Unique Qualities for Lasting Growth and Evolution.

"Only Dead Fish Flow with the Flow."

Make Success and Money a Consequence on What You Want to Do.

www.TheLazarElement.Com

RAKESH LAZAR

Mindset Coach – Communication Confidence

HR Business Consultant | ICF Certified Professional Coach (PCC) | Personal Transformation Facilitator | Thinking Partner for Senior Executives

www.ingramcontent.com/pod-product-compliance
Lightning Source LLC
LaVergne TN
LVHW021132200726
843510LV00001B/71